Immediatism

Essays by Hakim Bey

Graphics by Freddie Baer

&Anti-copyright, 1994. May be freely pirated and
quoted — the author and publisher, however, would
like to be informed at:

AK Press   AK Press
22 Lutton Place   P.O. Box 40682
Edinburgh, Scotland   San Francisco, CA
EH8 9PE   94140-0682

ISBN 1 873176 42 2

Library of Congress #94-79235

British Library Cataloguing in Publication Data

A catalogue record for this title is available from the
British Library.

First published as *Radio Sermonettes* (Libertarian Book
Club, New York, 1992) and republished with a new
preface in 1994 by:

AK Press   AK Press
22 Lutton Place   P.O. Box 40682
Edinburgh, Scotland   San Francisco, CA
EH8 9PE   94140-0682

Typeset, graphics and design donated by Freddie Baer.

Printed in the United States of America.

TABLE OF CONTENTS

ONTOLOGICAL ANARCHY
IN A NUTSHELL

Since absolutely nothing can be predicated with any real certainty as to the "true nature of things", all projects (as Nietzsche says) can only be "founded on nothing." And yet *there must be a project*—if only because we ourselves resist being categorized as "nothing." Out of nothing we will make something: the Uprising, the revolt against everything which proclaims: "The Nature of Things is such-&-such." We disagree, we are unnatural, we are less than nothing in the eyes of the Law — Divine Law, Natural Law, or Social Law — take your pick. Out of nothing we will imagine our *values*, and by this act of invention we shall live.

As we meditate on the *nothing* we notice that although it cannot be de-fined, nevertheless paradoxically we *can* say something about it (even if only metaphorically): — it appears to be a "chaos." Both as ancient myth and as "new science", chaos lies at the heart of our project. The great serpent (Tiamat, Python, Leviathan), Hesiod's primal Chaos, presides over the vast long dreaming of the Paleolithic — before all kings, priests, agents of Order, History, Hierarchy, Law. "Nothing" begins to take on a face — the smooth, featureless egg- or gourd-visage of Mr. Hun-Tun, chaos-as-becoming, chaos-as-excess, the generous outpouring of nothing into something.

In effect, chaos is life. All mess, all riot of color, all protoplasmic urgency, all *movement* — is chaos. From this point of view, Order appears as death, cessation, crystallization, alien silence.

Anarchists have been claiming for years that "anarchy is not chaos." Even anarchism seems to want a *natural law*, an inner and innate morality in matter, an entelechy or purpose-of-being. (No better than Christians in this respect, or so Nietzsche believed —radical only in the depth of their *resentment*.) Anarchism says that "the state should be abolished" only to institute a new more radical form of order in its place. Ontological Anarchy however replies that no "state" can "exist" in chaos, that all ontological claims are spurious except the claim of chaos (which however is undetermined), and therefore that governance of any sort is impossible. "Chaos never died." Any form of "order" which we have not imagined and produced directly and spontaneously in sheer "existential freedom" for our own celebratory purposes — is an illusion.

Of course, illusions can kill. Images of punishment haunt the sleep of Order. Ontological Anarchy proposes that we wake up, and create our own day — even in the shadow of the State, that pustulant giant who sleeps, and whose dreams of Order metastatize as spasms of spectacular violence.

The only force significant enough to facilitate our act of creation seems to be desire, or as Charles Fourier called it, "Passion." Just as Chaos and Eros (along with Earth and Old Night) are Hesiod's first deities, so too no human endeavor occurs outside their cosmogeneous circle of attraction.

The logic of Passion leads to the conclusion that all "states" are impossible, all "orders" illusory, except those of desire. No being, only becoming — hence the only viable government is that of love, or "attraction." Civilization merely hides from itself — behind a thin static scrim of rationality — the truth that only desire creates values. And so the values of Civilization are based on the denial of desire.

Capitalism, which claims to produce Order by means of the reproduction of desire, in fact originates in the production of *scarcity*, and can only reproduce itself in unfulfillment, negation, and alienation. As the Spectacle disintegrates (like a malfunctioning VR program) it reveals the fleshless bones of the Commodity. Like those tranced travelers in Irish fairy tales who visit the Otherworld and seem to dine on supernatural delicacies, we wake in a bleary dawn with ashes in our mouths.

Individual vs. Group — Self vs. Other — a false dichotomy propagated through the Media of Control, and above all through language. Hermes — the Angel — the medium is the Messenger. All forms of communicativeness should be angelic — language itself should be angelic — a kind of divine chaos. Instead it is infected with a self-replicating virus, an infinite crystal of separation, the *grammar* which prevents us from killing Nobodaddy once and for all.

Self and Other complement and complete one another. There is no Absolute Category, no Ego, no Society — but only a chaotically complex web of relation — and the "Strange Attractor", *attraction itself,* which evokes resonances and patterns in the flow of becoming.

Values arise from this turbulence, values which are based on abundance rather than scarcity, the gift rather than the commodity, and on the synergistic and mutual enhancement of individual and group; — values which are in every way the opposite of the morality and ethics of Civilization, because they have to do with life rather than death.

"Freedom is a psycho-kinetic skill" — not an abstract noun. A process, not a "state" — a movement, not a form of governance. The Land of the Dead knows that perfect Order from which the organic and animate shrink in horror — which explains why the Civilization of Slippage is more than half in love with easeful death. From Babylon and Egypt to the 20th Century, the architecture of Power can never quite be distinguished from the tumuli of the necropolis.

Nomadism, and the Uprising, provide us with possible models for an "everyday life" of Ontological Anarchy. The crystalline perfections of Civilization and Revolution cease to interest us when we have experienced them both as forms of War, variations on that tired old Babylonian Con, the myth of Scarcity. Like the bedouin we choose an architecture of skins — and an earth full of places of disappearance. Like the Commune, we choose a liquid space of celebration and risk rather than the icy waste of the Prism (or Prison) of Work, the economy of Lost Time, the rictus of nostalgia for a synthetic future.

A *utopian poetics* helps us to know our desires. The mirror of Utopia provides us with a kind of critical theory which no mere practical politics nor systematic philosophy can hope to evolve. But we have no time for theory which merely limits itself to the contemplation of utopia as "no-place place" while bewailing the "impossibility of desire." The penetration of everyday life by the marvelous — the creation of "situations" — belongs to the "material bodily principle", and to the imagination, and to the living fabric of the present.

The individual who realizes this immediacy can widen the circle of pleasure to some extent, simply by waking from the hypnosis of the "Spooks" (as Stirner called all abstractions); and yet more can be accomplished by "crime"; and still more by the doubling of the Self in sexuality. From Stirner's "Union of Self-Owning Ones" we proceed to Nietzsche's circle of "Free Spirits" and thence to Fourier's "Passional Series", doubling and re-doubling ourselves even as the Other multiplies itself in the *eros* of the group.

The activity of such a group will come to replace Art as we poor PoMo bastards know it. Gratuitous creativity, or "play", and the exchange of gifts, will cause the withering-away of Art as the reproduction of commodities. "Dada epistemology" will meltingly erase all separation, and give rebirth to a psychic paleolithism in which life and beauty can no longer be distinguished. Art in this sense has always been camouflaged and repressed throughout the whole of High History, but has never entirely vanished from our lives. One favorite example: — the *quilting bee* — a spontaneous patterning carried out by a non-hierarchic creative collective to produce a unique and useful and beautiful object, typically as a gift for someone connected to the circle.

The task of Immediatist organization can be summed up as the widening of this circle. The greater the portion of my life that can be wrenched from the Work/Consume/Die cycle, and (re)turned over to the economy of the "bee", the greater my chance for pleasure. One runs a certain risk in thus thwarting the vampiric energies of institutions. But risk itself makes up part of the direct experience of pleasure, a fact noted in all insurrectionary moments — all moments of waking-up — of intense adventurous enjoyments: — the festal aspect of the Uprising, the insurrectionary nature of the Festival.

But between the lonely awakening of the individual, and the synergetic anamnesis of the insurrectionary collectivity, there stretches out a whole spectrum of social forms with some potential for our "project". Some last no longer than a chance meeting between two kindred spirits who might enlarge each other by their brief and mysterious encounter; others are like holidays, still other like pirate utopias. None seems to last very long — but so what? Religions and States boasts of their *permanence* — which, we know, is just jive . . . ; what they mean is *death*.

We do not require "Revolutionary" *institutions*. "After the Revolution" we would still continue to drift, to evade the instant sclerosis of a politics of revenge, and instead seek out the excessive, the *strange* — which for us has become the sole possible norm. If we join or support certain "revolutionary" movements now, we'd certainly be the first to "betray" them if they "came to *power*". Power, after all, is for *us* — not some fucking vanguard party.

In *The Temporary Autonomous Zone* (Autonomedia, NY, 1991) there was a discussion of "the will to power as disappearance", emphasizing the evasive nature and ambiguity of the moment of "freedom". In the present series of texts (originally presented as Radio Sermonettes on an FM station in New York, and published under that title by the anarchist Libertarian Book Club), the focus shifts to the idea of a praxis of *re-appearance*, and thus to the problem of organization. An attempt at a theory of the aesthetics of the group — rather than a sociology or *politique* — has been expressed here as a game for free spirits, rather than as a blueprint for an institution. The group as medium, or as mechanism of alienation, has been replaced here by the Immediatist group, devoted to the overcoming of separation. This book might be called a thought-experiment on *festal sodality* — it has no higher ambitions. Above all, it does not pretend to know "what must be done" — the delusion of would-be commissars and gurus. It wants no disciples — it would prefer to be burned — immolation not emulation! In fact it has almost no interest in "dialogue" at all, and would prefer rather to attract co-conspirators than readers. It loves to talk, but only because talk is a kind of celebration rather than a kind of work.

And only intoxication stands between this book — and silence.

— Hakim Bey
(Vernal Equinox 1993)

IMMEDIATISM

i.

All experience is mediated — by the mechanisms of sense perception, mentation, language, etc. — & certainly all art consists of some further mediation of experience.

ii.

However, mediation takes place by degrees. Some experiences (smell, taste, sexual pleasure, etc.) are less mediated than others (reading a book, looking through a telescope, listening to a record). Some media, especially "live" arts such as dance, theater, musical or bardic performance, are less mediated than others such as TV, CDs, Virtual Reality. Even among the media usually called "media," some are more & others are less mediated, according to the intensity of imaginative participation they demand. Print & radio demand more of the imagination, film less, TV even less, VR the least of all — so far.

iii.

For art, the intervention of Capital always signals a further degree of mediation. To say that art is commodified is to say that a mediation, or standing-inbetween, has occurred, & that this betweenness amounts to a split, & that this split amounts to "alienation." Improv music played by friends at home is less "alienated" than music played "live" at the Met, or music played through media (whether PBS or MTV or Walkman). In fact, an argument could be made that music distributed free or at cost on cassette via mail is LESS alienated than live music played at some huge We Are The World spectacle or Las Vegas niteclub, even though the latter is live music played to a live audience (or at least so it appears), while the former is recorded music consumed by distant & even anonymous listeners.

iv.

The tendency of Hi Tech, & the tendency of Late Capitalism, both impel the arts farther & farther into extreme forms of mediation. Both widen the gulf between the production & consumption of art, with a corresponding increase in "alienation."

v.

With the disappearance of a "mainstream" & therefore of an "avant-garde" in the arts, it has been noticed that all the more advanced & intense art-experiences have been recuperable almost instantly by the media, & thus are rendered into trash like all other trash in the ghostly world of commodities. "Trash," as the term was redefined in, let's say, Baltimore in the 1970s, can be good fun — as an ironic take on a sort of inadvertent folkultur that surrounds & pervades the more unconscious regions of "popular" sensibility — which in turn is produced in part by the Spectacle. "Trash" was once a fresh concept, with radical potential. By now, however, amidst the ruins of Post-Modernism, it has finally begun to stink. Ironic frivolity finally becomes disgusting. Is it possible now to BE SERIOUS BUT NOT SOBER? (Note: The New Sobriety is of course simply the flipside of the New Frivolity. Chic neo-puritanism carries the taint of Reaction, in just the same way that postmodernist philosophical irony & despair lead to Reaction. The Purge Society is the same as the Binge Society. After the "12 steps" of trendy renunciation in the '90s, all that remains is the 13th step of the gallows. Irony may have become boring, but self-mutilation was never more than an abyss. Down with frivolity — Down with sobriety.)

Everything delicate & beautiful, from Surrealism to Break-dancing, ends up as fodder for McDeath's ads; 15 minutes later all the magic has been sucked out, & the art itself dead as a dried locust. The media-wizards, who are nothing if not postmodernists, have even begun to feed on the vitality of "Trash," like vultures regurgitating & re-consuming the same carrion, in an obscene ecstasy of self-referentiality. Which way to the Egress?

vi.

Real art is play, & play is one of the most immediate of all experiences. Those who have cultivated the pleasure of play cannot be expected to give it up simply to make a political point (as in an "Art Strike," or "the suppression *without* the realization" of art, etc.). Art will *go on,* in somewhat the same sense that breathing, eating, or fucking will go on.

vii.

Nevertheless, we are repelled by the extreme alienation of the arts, especially in "the media," in commercial publishing & galleries, in the recording "industry," etc. And we sometimes worry even about the extent to which our very involvement in such arts as writing, painting, or music implicates us in a nasty abstraction, a removal from immediate experience. We miss the directness of play (our original kick in doing art in the first place); we miss smell, taste, touch, the feel of bodies in motion.

viii.

Computers, video, radio, printing presses, synthesizers, fax machines, tape recorders, photocopiers — these things make good toys, but terrible addictions. Finally we realize we cannot "reach out & touch someone" who is not present in the flesh. These media may be useful to our art — but they must not possess us, nor must they stand between, mediate, or separate us from our animal/animate selves. We want to control our media, not be Controlled by them. And we should like to remember a certain psychic martial art which stresses the realization that the body itself is the least mediated of all media.

ix.

Therefore, as artists & "cultural workers" who have no intention of giving up activity in our chosen media, we nevertheless demand of ourselves an extreme awareness of *immediacy,* as well as the mastery of some direct means of implementing this awareness as play, immediately (at once) & immediately (without mediation).

x.

Fully realizing that any art "manifesto" written today can only stink of the same bitter irony it seeks to oppose, we nevertheless declare without hesitation (without too much thought) the founding of a "movement," IMMEDIATISM. We feel free to do so because we intend to practice Immediatism *in secret,* in order to avoid any contamination of mediation. Publicly we'll continue our work in publishing, radio, printing, music, etc., but privately we will create *something else,* something to be shared freely but never consumed passively, something which can be discussed openly but never understood by the agents of alienation, something with no commercial potential yet valuable beyond price, something occult yet woven completely into the fabric of our everyday lives.

xi.

Immediatism is not a movement in the sense of an aesthetic program. It depends on situation, not style or content, message or School. It may take the form of any kind of creative play which can be performed by two or more people, by & for themselves, face-to-face & together. In this sense it is like a game, & therefore certain "rules" may apply.

xii.

All spectators must also be performers. All expenses are to be shared, & all products which may result from the play are also to be shared by the participants only (who may keep them or bestow them as gifts, but should not sell them). The best games will make little or no use of obvious forms of mediation such as photography, recording, printing, etc., but will tend toward immediate techniques involving physical presence, direct communication, & the senses.

xiii.

An obvious matrix for Immediatism is the party. Thus a good meal could be an Immediatist art project, especially if everyone present cooked as well as ate. Ancient Chinese & Japanese on misty autumn days would hold odor parties, where each guest would bring a homemade incense or perfume. At linked-verse parties a faulty couplet would entail the penalty of a glass of wine. Quilting bees, *tableaux vivants*, exquisite corpses, rituals of conviviality like Fourier's "Museum Orgy" (erotic costumes, poses, & skits), live music & dance — the past can be ransacked for appropriate forms, & imagination will supply more.

xiv.

The difference between a 19th century quilting bee, for example, & an Immediatist quilting bee would lie in our awareness of the practice of Immediatism as a response to the sorrows of alienation & the "death of art."

xv.

The mail art of the '70s & the zine scene of the '80s were attempts to go beyond the mediation of art-as-commodity, & may be considered ancestors of Immediatism.

11

However, they preserved the mediated structures of postal communication & xerography, & thus failed to overcome the isolation of the players, who remained quite literally out of touch. We wish to take the motives & discoveries of these earlier movements to their logical conclusion in an art which banishes all mediation & alienation, at least to the extent that the human condition allows.

xvi.

Moreover, Immediatism is not condemned to powerlessness in the world, simply because it avoids the publicity of the marketplace. "Poetic Terrorism" & "Art Sabotage" are quite logical manifestations of Immediatism.

xvii.

Finally, we expect that the practice of Immediatism will release within us vast storehouses of forgotten power, which will not only transform our lives through the secret realization of unmediated play, but will also inescapably well up & burst out & permeate the *other* art we create, the more public & mediated art.

And we hope that the two will grow closer & closer, & eventually perhaps become one.

THE TONG

*The mandarins draw their power from the law;
the people from the secret societies.*

(Chinese saying)

Last winter I read a book on the Chinese Tongs *(Primitive Revolutionaries of China: A Study of Secret Societies in the Late Nineteenth Century,* Fei-Ling Davis; Honolulu, 1971-77): — maybe the first ever written by someone who *wasn't* a British Secret Service agent! — (in fact, she was a Chinese socialist who died young — this was her only book) — & for the first time I realized why I've always been attracted to the Tong: not just for the romanticism, the elegant decadent chinoiserie decor, as it were — but also for the form, the structure, the very essence of the thing.

Some time later in an excellent interview with William Burroughs in *Homocore* magazine I discovered that he too has become fascinated with Tongs & suggests the form as a perfect mode of organization for queers, particularly in this present era of shitheel moralism & hysteria. I'd agree, & extend the recommendation to *all* marginal groups, especially ones whose jouissance involves illegalism (potheads, sex heretics, insurrectionists) or extreme eccentricity (nudists, pagans, post-avant-garde artists, etc., etc.).

A Tong can perhaps be defined as a mutual benefit society for people with a common interest which is illegal or dangerously marginal — hence, the necessary *secrecy.* Many Chinese Tongs revolved around smuggling & tax-evasion, or clandestine self-control of certain trades (in opposition to State control), or insurrectionary political or religious aims (overthrow of the Manchus for example — several tongs collaborated with the Anarchists in the 1911 Revolution).

A common purpose of the tongs was to collect & invest membership dues & initiation fees in insurance funds for the indigent, unemployed, widows & orphans of deceased members, funeral expenses, etc. In an era like ours when the poor are caught between the cancerous Scylla of the insurance industry & the fast-evaporating Charybdis of welfare & public health services, this purpose of the Secret Society might well regain its appeal. (Masonic lodges were organized on this basis, as were the early & illegal trade unions & "chivalric orders" for laborers & artisans.) Another universal purpose for such societies was of course conviviality, especially banqueting — but even this apparently innocuous pastime can acquire insurrectionary implications. In the various French revolutions, for example, dining clubs frequently took on the role of radical organizations when all other forms of public meeting were banned.

Recently I talked about tongs with "P.M.," author of *bolo'bolo* (Semiotext(e) Foreign Agents Series). I argued that secret societies are once again a valid possibility for groups seeking autonomy & individual realization. He disagreed, but not (as I expected) because of the "elitist" connotations of secrecy. He felt that such organizational forms work best for already-close-knit groups with strong economic, ethnic/regional, or religious ties — conditions which do not exist (or exist only embryonically) in today's marginal scene. He proposed instead the establishment of multi-purpose neighborhood centers, with expenses to be shared by various special-interest groups & small-entrepreneurial concerns (craftspeople, coffeehouses, performance spaces, etc.). Such large centers would require official status (State recognition), but would obviously become foci for all sorts of non-official activity — black markets, temporary organization for "protest" or insurrectionary action, uncontrolled "leisure" & unmonitored conviviality, etc.

In response to "P.M."'s critique I have not abandoned but rather modified my concept of what a modern Tong might be. The intensely hierarchical structure of the traditional tong would obviously not work, although some of the forms could be saved & used in the same way titles & honors are used in our "free religions" (or "weird" religions, "joke" religions, anarcho-neo-pagan cults, etc.). Non-hierarchic organization appeals to us, but so too does ritual, incense, the delightful bombast of occult orders — "Tong Aesthetics" you might call it — so why shouldn't we have our cake & eat it too? — (especially if it's Moroccan *majoun* or *baba au absinthe* — something a bit *forbidden!*). Among other things, the Tong should be a work of art.

The strict traditional rule of secrecy also needs modification. Nowadays anything which evades the idiot gaze of publicity is already *virtually* secret. Most modern people seem unable to believe in the reality of something they never see on television — therefore to escape being televisualized is already to be quasi-invisible. Moreover, that which is seen through the mediation of the media becomes somehow unreal, & loses its power (I won't bother to defend this thesis but simply refer the reader to a train of thought which leads from Nietzsche to Benjamin to Bataille to Barthes to Foucault to Baudrillard). By contrast, perhaps that which is *unseen* retains its reality, its rootedness in everyday life & therefore in the possibility of the marvelous.

So the modern Tong cannot be elitist — but there's no reason it can't be *choosy.* Many non-authoritarian organizations have foundered on the dubious principle of open membership, which frequently leads to a preponderance of assholes, yahoos, spoilers, whining neurotics, & police agents. If a Tong is organized around a special interest (especially an illegal or risky or marginal interest) it certainly has the right to compose itself according to the "affinity group" principle. If secrecy means (a) avoiding publicity & (b) vetting possible members, the "secret society" can scarcely be accused of violating anarchist principles. In fact, such societies have a long & honorable history in the antiauthoritarian movement, from Proudhon's dream of re-animating the Holy Vehm as a kind of "People's Justice," to Bakunin's various schemes, to Durutti's "Wanderers." We ought not to allow marxist historians to convince us that such expedients are "primitive" & have therefore been left behind by "History." The absoluteness of "History" is at best a dubious proposition. We are not interested in a return to the primitive, but in a return OF the primitive, inasmuch as the primitive is the "repressed."

In the old days secret societies would appear in times & spaces forbidden by the State, i.e. where & when people are *kept apart* by law. In our times people are usually not kept apart by law but by mediation & alienation (see Part 1, "Immediatism"). Secrecy therefore becomes an avoidance of mediation, while conviviality changes from a secondary to a primary purpose of the "secret society." Simply to meet together face-to-face is already an action against the forces which oppress us by isolation, by loneliness, by the trance of media.

In a society which enforces a schizoid split between Work & Leisure, we have all experienced the trivialization of our "free time," time which is organized neither as work nor as leisure. ("Vacation" once meant "empty" time — now it signifies time which is organized & filled by the industry of leisure.) The "secret" purpose of conviviality in the secret society then becomes the self-structuring & auto-valorization of free time. Most parties are devoted only to loud music & too much booze, not because we enjoy them but because the Empire of Work has imbued us with the feeling that empty time is wasted time. The idea of throwing a party to, say, make a quilt or sing madrigals together, seems hopelessly outdated. But the modern Tong will find it both necessary & enjoyable to seize back free time from the commodity world & devote it to shared creation, to *play*.

I know of several societies organized along these lines already, but I'm certainly not going to blow their secrecy by discussing them in print. There are *some* people who do not need fifteen seconds on the Evening News to validate their existence. Of course, the marginal press & radio (probably the only media in which this sermonette will appear) are practically invisible anyway — certainly still quite opaque to the gaze of Control. Nevertheless, there's the principle of the thing: secrets should be respected. Not everyone needs to know everything! What the 20th century lacks most—& needs most—is *tact*. We wish to replace democratic epistemology with "dada epistemology" (Feyerabend). Either you're on the bus or you're not on the bus.

Some will call this an elitist attitude, but it is not — at least not in the C. Wright Mills sense of the word: that is, a small group which exercises power over non-insiders for its own aggrandizement. Immediatism does not concern itself with power-relations; — It desires neither to be ruled nor to rule. The contemporary Tong therefore finds no pleasure in the degeneration of institutions into conspiracies. It wants power for its own purposes of mutuality. It is a free association of individuals who have chosen each other as the subjects of the group's generosity, its "expansiveness" (to use a sufi term). If this amounts to some kind of "elitism," then so be it.

If Immediatism begins with groups of friends trying not just to overcome isolation but also to enhance each other's lives, soon it will want to take a more complex shape: — nuclei of mutually-self-chosen allies, working (playing) to occupy more & more time & space outside all mediated structure & control. Then it will want to become a horizontal network of such autonomous groups — then, a "tendency" — then, a "movement" — then, a kinetic web of "temporary autonomous zones." At last it will strive to become the kernel of a new society, giving birth to itself within the corrupt shell of the old. For all these purposes the secret society promises to provide a useful framework of protective clandestinity — a cloak of invisibility that will have to be dropped only in the event of some final showdown with the Babylon of Mediation . . .

Prepare for the Tong Wars!

IMMEDIATISM VS. CAPITALISM

Many monsters stand between us & the realization of Immediatist goals. For instance our own ingrained unconscious alienation might all too easily be mistaken for a virtue, especially when contrasted with crypto-authoritarian pap passed off as "community," or with various upscale versions of "leisure." Isn't it natural to take the *dandyism noir* of curmudgeonly hermits for some kind of heroic individualism, when the only visible contrast is Club Med commodity socialism, or the gemutlich masochism of the Victim Cults? To be doomed & cool naturally appeals more to noble souls than to be saved & cozy.

Immediatism means to enhance individuals by providing a matrix of friendship, not to belittle them by sacrificing their "ownness" to group-think, leftist self-abnegation, or New Age clone-values. What must be overcome is not individuality per se, but rather the addiction to bitter loneliness which characterizes consciousness in the 20th century (which is by & large not much more than a re-run of the 19th).

Far more dangerous than any inner monster of (what might be called) "negative selfishness," however, is the outward, very real & utterly objective monster of too-Late Capitalism. The marxists (R.I.P.) had their own version of how this worked, but here we are not concerned with abstract/dialectical analyses of labor-value or class structure (even though these may still require analysis, & even more so since the "death" or "disappearance" of Communism). Instead we'd like to point out specific tactical dangers facing any Immediatist project.

1. Capitalism only *supports* certain kinds of groups, the nuclear family for example, or "the people I know at my job," because such groups are already self-alienated & hooked into the Work/Consume/Die structure. Other kinds of groups may be *allowed*, but will lack all support from the societal structure, & thus find themselves facing grotesque challenges & difficulties which appear under the guise of "bad luck."

The first & most innocent-seeming obstacle to any Immediatist project will be the "busyness" or "need to make a living" faced by each of its associates. However there is no real innocence here — only our profound ignorance of the ways is which Capitalism itself is organized to prevent all genuine conviviality.

No sooner have a group of friends begun to visualize immediate goals realizable only thru solidarity & cooperation, when suddenly one of them will be offered a "good" job in Cincinnati or teaching English in Taiwan — or else have to move back to California to care for a dying parent — or else they'll lose the "good" job they already have & be reduced to a state of misery which precludes their very enjoyment of the group's project or goals (i.e. they'll become "depressed"). At the most mundane-seeming level, the group will fail to agree on a day of the week for meetings because everyone is "busy." But this is not mundane. It's sheer cosmic evil. We whip ourselves into froths of indignation over "oppression" & "unjust laws" when in fact these abstractions have little impact on our daily lives — while that which really makes us miserable goes unnoticed, written off to "busyness" or "distraction" or even to the nature of reality itself ("Well, I can't *live* without a job").

Yes, perhaps it's true we can't "live" without a job — although I hope we're grown-up enough to know the difference between *life* & the accumulation of a bunch of fucking *gadgets*. Still, we must constantly remind ourselves (since our culture won't do it for us) that this monster called WORK remains the precise & exact target of our rebellious wrath, the one single most oppressive *reality* we face (& we must learn also to recognize Work when it's disguised as "leisure").

To be "too busy" for the Immediatist project is to miss the very essence of Immediatism. To struggle to *come together* every Monday night (or whatever), in the teeth of the gale of busyness, or family, or invitations to stupid parties — that struggle is *already* Immediatism itself. Succeed in actually physically meeting face-to-face with a group which is not your spouse-&-kids, or the "guys from my job," or your 12-step Program — & you have *already* achieved virtually everything Immediatism yearns for. An actual project will arise almost spontaneously out of this successful slap-in-the-face of the social norm of alienated boredom. Outwardly, of course, the project will seem to be the group's purpose, its motive for coming together — but in fact the opposite is true. We're not kidding or indulging in hyperbole when we insist that *meeting-face-to-face is already "the revolution."* Attain it & the creativity part comes naturally; like "the kingdom of heaven" it will be added unto you. Of *course* it will be horribly difficult — why else would we have spent the last decade trying to construct our "bohemia in the mail," if it were easy to have it in some *quartier latin* or rural commune? The rat-bastard Capitalist scum who are telling you to "reach out & touch someone" with a telephone or "be there!" (where? alone in front of a goddam television??) — these lovecrafty suckers are trying to turn you into a scrunched-up blood-drained pathetic crippled little cog in the death-machine of the human soul (& let's not have any theological quibbles about what we mean by "soul"!). Fight them — by meeting with friends, not to consume or produce, but to enjoy friendship — & you will have triumphed (at least for a moment) over the most pernicious conspiracy in EuroAmerican society today — the conspiracy to turn you into a living corpse galvanized by prosthesis & the terror of scarcity — to turn you into a spook haunting your own brain. This is not a petty matter! This is a question of failure or triumph!

2. If busyness & fissipation are the first potential failures of Immediatism, we cannot say that its triumph should be equated with "success." The second major threat to our project can quite simply be described as the tragic success of the project itself. Let's say we've overcome physical alienation & have actually met, developed our project, & created something (a quilt, a banquet, a play, a bit of eco-sabotage, etc.). Unless we keep it an absolute secret — which is probably impossible & in any case would constitute a somewhat poisonous selfishness — *other people* will hear of it (other people from hell, to paraphrase the existentialists) — & among these other people, some will be agents (conscious or unconscious, it doesn't matter) of too-Late Capitalism. The Spectacle — or whatever has replaced it since 1968 — is above all *empty*. It fuels itself by the constant Moloch-like gulping-down of everyone's creative powers & ideas. It's more desperate for *your* "radical subjectivity" than any vampire or cop for your blood. It wants your creativity much more even than you want it yourself. It would die unless you desired it, & you will only desire it if it seems to offer you the very desires you dreamed, alone in your lonely genius, disguised & sold back to you as commodities. Ah, the metaphysical shenanigans of objects! (or words to that effect, Marx cited by Benjamin).

Suddenly it will appear to you (as if a demon had whispered it in your ear) that the Immediatist art you've created is so good, so fresh, so original, so strong compared to all the crap on the "market" — so *pure* — that you could water it down & sell it, & *make a* living at it, so you could all knock off WORK, buy a farm in the country, & do art together for-ever after. And perhaps it's true. You *could* . . . after all, you're geniuses. But it'd be better to fly to Hawaii & throw yourself into a live volcano. Sure, you could have success; you could even have 15 seconds on the Evening News — or a PBS documentary made on your life. Yes indeed.

3. But this is where the last major monster steps in, crashes thru the living room wall, & snuffs you (if Success itself hasn't already "spoiled" you, that is).

Because in order to succeed you must first be "seen." And if you are *seen*, you will be perceived as wrong, illegal, immoral—different. The Spectacle's main sources of creative energy are all in prison. If you're not a nuclear family or a guided tour or the Republican Party, then why are you meeting every Monday evening? To do drugs? illicit sex? income tax evasion? satanism?

And of course the chances are good that your Immediatist group *is* engaged in something illegal — since almost everything enjoyable is in fact illegal. Babylon hates it when anyone actually enjoys life, rather than merely spends money in a vain attempt to buy the illusion of enjoyment. Dissipation, gluttony, bulimic overconsumption — these are not only legal but mandatory. If you don't waste yourself on the emptiness of commodities you are obviously *queer* & must by definition be breaking some law. True pleasure in this society is more dangerous than bank robbery. At least bank robbers share Massa's respect for Massa's money. But you, you perverts, clearly deserve to be burned at the stake — & here come the peasants with their torches, eager to do the State's bidding without even being asked. Now you are the monsters, & your little gothic castle of Immediatism is engulfed in flames. Suddenly cops are swarming out of the woodwork. Are your papers in order? Do you have a permit to exist?

Immediatism is a picnic — but it's not *easy*. Immediatism is the most natural path for free humans imaginable—& *therefore* the most unnatural abomination in the eyes of Capital. Immediatism will triumph, but only at the cost of *self-organization of power, of clandestinity, & of insurrection*. Immediatism is our delight, Immediatism is *dangerous*.

INVOLUTION

So far we've treated Immediatism as an aesthetic movement rather than a political one—but if the "personal is political" then certainly the aesthetic must be considered even more so. "Art for art's sake" cannot really be said to exist at all, unless it be taken to imply that art *per se* functions as political power, i.e. power capable of expressing or even changing the world rather than merely describing it.

In fact art always seeks such power, whether the artist remains unconscious of the fact & believes in "pure" aesthetics, or becomes so hyper-conscious of the fact as to produce nothing but agit-prop. Consciousness in itself, as Nietzsche pointed out, plays a less significant role in life than power. No snappier proof of this could be imagined than the continued existence of an "Art World" (SoHo, 57th St., etc.) which still believes in the separate realms of political art & aesthetic art. Such failure of consciousness allows this "world" the luxury of producing art with overt political *content* (to satisfy their liberal customers) as well as art without such content, which merely expresses the power of the bourgeois scum & bankers who buy it for their investment portfolios.

If art did not possess & wield this power it would not be worth doing & nobody would do it. Literal art for art's sake would produce nothing but impotence & nullity. Even the fin-de-siécle decadents who invented *l'art pour l'art* used it politically: — as a weapon against bourgeois values of "utility," "morality" & so on. The idea that art can be voided of political meaning appeals now only to those liberal cretins who wish to excuse "pornography" or other forbidden aesthetic games on the grounds that "it's only art" & hence can change nothing. (I hate these assholes worse than Jesse Helms; at least *he* still believes that art has *power!)*

Even if an art without political content can — for the moment— be admitted to exist (altho this remains exceedingly problematic), then the political meaning of art can still be sought in the *means of its production & consumption*. The art of 57th St. remains bourgeois no matter how radical its content may appear, as Warhol proved by painting Che Guevara; in fact Valerie Solanis revealed herself far more radical than Warhol—by shooting him —(& perhaps even more radical than Che, that Rudolf Valentino of Red Fascism).

In fact we're not terribly concerned with the content of Immediatist art. Immediatism remains for us more game than "movement"; as such, the game might result in Brechtian didacticism or Poetic Terrorism, but it might equally well leave behind no content at all (as in a banquet), or else one with no obvious political message (such as a quilt). The radical quality of Immediatism expresses itself rather in its mode of production & consumption.

That is, it is produced by a group of friends either for itself alone or for a larger circle of friends; it is *not* produced for sale, nor is it sold, nor (ideally) is it allowed to slip out of the control of its producers in any way. If it is meant for consumption outside the circle then it must be made in such a way as to remain impervious to cooptation & commodification. For example, if one of our quilts escaped us & ended up sold as "art" to some capitalist or museum, we should consider it a disaster. Quilts must remain in our hands or be given to those who will appreciate them & keep them. As for our agitprop, it must resist commodification by its very form; — we don't want our posters sold twenty years later as "art," like Myakovsky (or Brecht, for that matter). The best Immediatist agitprop will leave no trace at all, except in the souls of those who are *changed* by it.

Let us repeat here that participation in Immediatism does not preclude the production/consumption of art in other ways by the individuals making up the group. We are not ideologues, & this is not Jonestown. This is a game, not a movement; it has rules of play, but no laws. Immediatism would love it if everyone were an artist. but our goal is not mass conversion. The game's payoff lies in its ability to escape the paradoxes & contradictions of the commercial art world (including literature, etc.), in which all liberatory gestures seem to end up as mere representations & hence betrayals of themselves. We offer the chance for art which is immediately *present* by virtue of the fact that it can exist only in our presence. Some of us may still write novels or paint pictures, either to "make a living" or to seek out ways to redeem these forms from recuperation. But Immediatism sidesteps both these problems. Thus it is "privileged," like all games.

But we cannot for this reason alone call it *involuted*, turned in on itself, closed, hermetic, elitist, art for art's sake. In Immediatism art is produced & consumed in a certain way, & this modus operandi is already "political" in a very specific sense. In order to grasp this sense, however, we must first explore "involution" more closely.

It's become a truism to say that society no longer expresses a consensus (whether reactionary or liberatory), but that a false consensus is expressed for society; let's call this false consensus "the Totality." The Totality is produced thru mediation & alienation, which attempt to subsume or absorb all creative energies for the Totality. Myakovsky killed himself when he realized this; perhaps we're made of sterner stuff, perhaps not. But for the sake of argument, let us assume that suicide is *not* a "solution."

The Totality isolates individuals & renders them powerless by offering only illusory modes of social expression, modes which seem to promise liberation or self-fulfillment but in fact end by producing yet more mediation & alienation. This complex can be viewed clearly at the level of "commodity fetishism," in which the most rebellious or avant-garde forms in art can be turned into fodder for PBS or MTV or ads for jeans or perfume.

On a subtler level, however, the Totality can absorb & re-direct any power whatsoever simply by re-contextualizing & re-presenting it. For instance< the liberatory power of a painting can be neutralized or even absorbed simply by placing it in the context of a gallery or museum, where it will automatically become a mere *representation* of liberatory power. The insurrectionary gesture of a madman or criminal is not negated only by locking up the perpetrator, but even more by allowing the gesture to be represented — by a psychiatrist or by some brainless Kop-show on channel 5 or even by a coffee-table book on Art Brut. This has been called "Spectacular recuperation"; however, the Totality can go even farther than this simply by *simulating* that which it formerly sought to recuperate. That is, the artist & madman are no longer necessary even as sources of appropriation or "mechanical reproduction," as Benjamin called it. Simulation cannot reproduce the faint reflection of "aura" which Benjamin allowed even to commodity-trash, its "utopian trace." Simulation cannot in fact reproduce or produce anything except desolation & misery. But since the Totality *thrives* on our misery, simulation suits its purpose quite admirably.

All these effects can be tracked most obviously & crudely in the area generally called "the Media" (altho we contend that *mediation* has a much wider range than even the term *broad-cast* could ever describe or indicate). The role of the Media in the recent Nintendo War — in fact the Media's one-to-one identification with that war — provides a perfect & exemplary scenario. All over America millions of people possessed *at least* enough "enlightenment" to condemn this hideous parody of morality enforced by that murderous crack-dealing spy in the White House. The Media however produced (i.e. simulated) the impression that virtually no opposition to Bush's war existed or could exist; that (to quote Bush) "there is no Peace Movement." And is fact there *was* no Peace *Movement* —only millions of people whose desire for peace had been *negated by the Totality,* wiped out, "disappeared" like victims of Peruvian death squads; people separated from each other by the brutal alienation of TV, news management, infotainment & sheer disinformation; people made to feel isolated, alienated, weird, queer, wrong, finally non-existent; people without voices; people without power.

This process of fragmentation has reached near-universal completion in our society, at least in the area of social discourse. Each person engages in a "relation of involution" with the spectacular simulation of Media. That is, our "relation" with Media is essentially empty & illusory, so that even when we seem to reach out & perceive reality in Media, we are in fact merely driven back in upon ourselves, alienated, isolated, & impotent. America is full to overflowing with people who feel that no matter what they say or do, no difference will be made; that no one is listening; that there is no one to listen. This *feeling* is the triumph of the Media. "They" speak, *you* listen — & therefore turn in upon yourself in a spiral of loneliness, distraction, depression, & spiritual death.

This process affects not only individuals but also such groups as still exist outside the Consensus Matrix of nuke-family, school, church, job, army, political party, etc. Each *group* of artists or peace activists or whatever is also made to feel that no contact with other groups is possible. Each "life-style" group buys the simulation of rivalry & enmity with other such groups of consumers. Each class & race is assured of its ungulfable existential alienation from all other classes & races (as in *Lifestyles of the Rich & Famous*).

The concept of "networking" began as a revolutionary strategy to bypass & overcome the Totality by setting up horizontal connections (unmediated by authority) among individuals & groups. In the 1980s we discovered that networking could also be mediated & in fact had to be mediated — by telephone, computers, the post office, etc. — & thus was doomed to fail us in our struggle against alienation. Communication technology may still prove to offer useful *tools* in this struggle, but by now it has become clear that CommTech is not a goal in itself. And in fact our distrust of seemingly "democratic" tech like PCs & phones increases with every revolutionary failure to hold control of the means of production. Frankly we do not wish to be forced to make up our minds whether or not any new tech will be or must be either liberatory or counter-liberatory. "After the revolution" such questions would answer themselves in the context of a "politics of desire." For the time being, however, we have discovered (not invented) Immediatism as a means of direct production & presentation of creative, liberatory & ludic energies, carried out without recourse to mediation of any mechanistic or alienated structures *whatsoever . . .* or at least so we hope.

In other words, whether or not any given technology or form of mediation can be used to overcome the Totality, we have decided to play a game that uses no such tech & hence does not need to question it — at least, not within the borders of the game. We reserve our challenge, our question, for the total Totality, not for any one "issue" with which it seeks to distract us.

And this brings us back to the "political form" of Immediatism. Face-to-face, body-to-body, breath-to breath (literally a conspiracy) — the game of Immediatism simply *cannot* be played on any level accessible to the false Consensus. It does not represent "everyday life" — *it cannot BE other than everyday life*, although it positions itself for the penetration of the marvelous, for the illumination of the real by the wonderful. Like a secret society, the networking it does must be slow (infinitely more slow than the "pure speed" of CommTech, media & war), & it must be *corporeal* rather than abstract, fleshless, mediated by machine or by authority or by simulation.

In this sense we say that Immediatism is a picnic (a conviviality) but is not *easy* — that it is most natural for free spirits but that it is *dangerous*. Content has nothing to do with it. The sheer existence of Immediatism is already an insurrection.

Imagination

There is a time for the theatre. — If people's imagination grows weak there arises in it the inclination to have its legends presented to it on the stage: it can now endure these crude substitutes for imagination. But for those ages to which the epic rhapsodist belongs, the theatre and the actor disguised as a hero is a hindrance to imagination rather than a means of giving it wings: too close, too definite, too heavy, too little in it of dream and bird-flight.

— Nietzsche

But of course the rhapsodist, who here appears only one step removed from the shaman (" . . . dream and bird-flight") must also be called a kind of *medium* or bridge standing between "a people" and its imagination. (Note: we'll use the word "imagination" sometimes in Wm. Blake's sense & sometimes in Gaston Bachelard's sense without opting for either a "spiritual" or an "aesthetic" determination, & without recourse to metaphysics.) A bridge carries across ("translate," "metaphor") but is not the original. And to translate is to betray. Even the rhapsodist provides a little poison for the imagination.

Ethnography, however, allows us to assert the possibility of societies where shamans are not *specialists* of the imagination, but where everyone is a special sort of shaman. In these societies, all members (except the psychically handicapped) act as shamans & bards for themselves as well as for their people. For example: certain Amerindian tribes of the Great Plains developed the most complex of all hunter/gatherer societies quite late in their history (perhaps partly in thanks to the gun & horse, technologies adopted from European culture). Each person acquired complete identity & full membership in "the People" only thru the Vision Quest, & its artistic enactment for the tribe. Thus each person became an "epic rhapsodist" in sharing this individuality with the collectivity.

The Pygmies, among the most "primitive" cultures, neither produce nor consume their music, but become *en masse* "the Voice of the Forest." At the other end of the scale, among complex agricultural societies, like Bali on the verge of the 20th century, "everyone is an artist" (& in 1980 a Javanese mystic told me, "Everyone *must be* an artist!).

The goals of Immediatism lie somewhere along the trajectory described roughly by these three points (Pygmies, Plains Indians, Balinese), which have all been linked to the anthropological concept of "democratic shamanism." Creative acts, themselves the outer results of the inwardness of imagination, are not *mediated & alienated* (in the sense we've been using those terms) when they are carried out BY everyone FOR everyone — when they are produced but not reproduced — when they are shared but not fetishized. Of course these acts are achieved thru mediation of some sort & to some extent, as are all acts — but they have not yet become forces of extreme alienation between some Expert/Priest/Producer on the one hand & some hapless "layperson" or consumer on the other.

Different media therefore exhibit different degrees of mediation — & perhaps they can even be ranked on that basis. Here everything depends on reciprocity, on a more-or-less equal exchange of what may be called "quanta of imagination." In the case of the epic rhapsodist who mediates vision for the tribe, a great deal of work — or active dreaming — still remains to be done by the hearers. They must participate imaginatively in the act of telling/hearing, & must call up images from their own stores of creative power to complete the rhapsodist's act.

In the case of Pygmy music the reciprocity becomes nearly as complete as possible, since the entire tribe mediates vision only & precisely for the entire tribe; — while for the Balinese, reciprocity assumes a more complex economy is which specialization is highly articulated, in which "the artist is not a special kind of person, but each person is a special kind of artist."

In the "ritual theater" of Voodoo & Santeria, everyone present must participate by visualizing the loas or orishas (imaginal archetypes), & by calling upon them (with "signature" chants & rhythms) to manifest. Anyone present may become a "horse" or medium for one of these *santos*, whose words & actions then assume for all celebrants the aspect of the presence of the spirit (i.e. the possessed person does not represent but presents). This structure, which also underlies Indonesian ritual theater, may be taken as exemplary for the creative production of "democratic shamanism." In order to construct our scale of imagination for all media, we may start by comparing this "voodoo theater" with the 18th century European theater described by Nietzsche.

In the latter, nothing of the original vision (or "spirit") is actually present. The actors merely re-present — they are "disguised." It is not expected that any member of troupe or audience will suddenly become possessed (or even "inspired" to any great extent) by the playwright's images. The actors are specialists or experts of representation, while the audience are "laypeople" to whom various images are being transferred. The audience is passive, too much is being done for the audience, who are indeed locked in place in darkness & silence, immobilized by the money they've paid for this vicarious experience.

Artaud, who realized this, attempted to revive ritual voodoo theater (banished from Western Culture by Aristotle) — but he carried out the attempt within the very structure (actor/audience) of aristotelian theater; he tried to destroy or mutate it from the inside out. He failed

& went insane, setting off a whole series of experiments which culminated in the Living Theater's assault on the actor/audience barrier, a literal assault which tried to force audience members to "participate" in the ritual. These experiments produced some great theater, but all failed in their deepest purpose. None managed to overcome the alienation Nietzsche & Artaud had criticized.

Even so, Theater occupies a much higher place on the imaginal Scale than other & later media such as film. At least in theater actors & audience are physically present in the same space together, allowing for the creation of what Peter Brook calls the "invisible golden chain" of attention & fellow-feeling between actors & audience — the well-known "magic" of theater. With film, however, this chain is broken. Now the audience sits alone in the dark with nothing to do, while the absent actors are represented by gigantic icons. Always the same no matter how many times it is "shown," made to be reproduced mechanically, devoid of all "aura," film actually *forbids* its audience to "participate" — film has no need of the audience's imagination. Of course, film does need the audience's money, & money is a kind of concretized imaginal residue, after all.

Eisenstein would point out that montage establishes a dialectic tension in film which engages the viewer's mind — intellect & imagination — & Disney might add (if he were capable of ideology) that animation increases this effect because animation is, is effect, completely made up of montage. Film too has its "magic." Granted. But from the point of view of *structure* we have come a long way from voodoo theater & democratic shamanism — we have come perilously close to the commodification of the imagination, & to the alienation of commodity-relations. We have almost resigned our power of flight, even of dream-flight.

Books? Books as media transmit only words — no sounds, sights, smells or feels, all of which are left up to the reader's imagination. Fine . . . But there's nothing "democratic" about books. The author/publisher produces, you consume. Books appeal to "imaginative" people, perhaps, but all their imaginal activity really amounts to passivity, sitting alone with a book, letting someone else tell the story. The magic of books has something sinister about it, as in Borges's Library. The Church's idea of a list of damnable books probably didn't go far enough — for in a sense, all books are damned. The *eros* of the text is a perversion — albeit, nevertheless, one to which *we* are addicted, & in no hurry to kick.

As for radio, it is clearly a medium of absence — like the book only more so, since books leave you alone in the light, radio alone in the dark. The more exacerbated passivity of the "listener" is revealed by the fact that advertisers pay for spots on radio, not in books (or not very much). Nevertheless radio leaves a great deal more imaginative "work" for the listener than, say, television for the viewer. The magic of radio: one can use it to listen to sunspot radiation, storms on Jupiter, the whizz of comets. Radio is old-fashioned; therein lies its seductiveness. Radio preachers say, "Put your haaands on the Radio, brothers & sisters, & feel the heeeeaaaling power of the *Word!*" Voodoo Radio?

(Note: A similar analysis of recorded music might be made: i.e., that it is alienating but not yet alienated. Records replaced family amateur music-making. Recorded music is too ubiquitous, too easy — that which is not present is not *rare*. And yet there's a lot to be said for scratchy old 78s played over distant radio stations late at night — a flash of illumination which seems to spark across all the levels of mediation & achieve a paradoxical presence.)

It's in this sense that we might perhaps give some credence to the otherwise dubious proposition that "radio is good — television evil!" For television occupies the bottom rung of the scale of imagination in media.

No, that's not true. "Virtual Reality" is even lower. But TV is the medium the Situationists meant when they referred to "the Spectacle." Television is the medium which Immediatism most wants to overcome. Books, theater, film & radio all retain what Benjamin called "the utopian trace" (at least in *potential*) — the last vestige of an impulse against alienation, the last perfume of the imagination. TV however *began* by erasing even that trace. No wonder the first broadcasters of video were the Nazis. TV is to the imagination what virus is to the DNA. The end. Beyond TV there lies only the infra-media realm of no-space/no-time, the instantaneity & ecstasis of CommTech, pure speed, the downloading of consciousness into the machine, into the program — in other words, hell.

Does this mean that Immediatism wants to "abolish television"? No, certainly not — for Immediatism wants to be a game, not a political movement, & certainly not a revolution with the power to abolish any medium. The goals of Immediatism must be positive, not negative. We feel no calling to eliminate any "means of production" (or even re-production) which might after all some day fall into the hands of "a people."

We have analyzed media by asking how much imagination is involved in each, & how much reciprocity, solely in order to implement for ourselves the most effective means of solving the problem outlined by Nietzsche & felt so painfully by Artaud, the problem of alienation. For this task we need a rough hierarchy of media, a means of measuring their potential for our uses. Roughly, then, *the more imagination is liberated & shared, the more useful the medium.*

Perhaps we can no longer call up spirits to possess us, or visit their realms as the shamans did. Perhaps no such spirits exist, or perhaps we are too "civilized" to recognize them. Or perhaps not. The creative imagination, however, remains for us a reality — & one which we must explore, even in the vain hope of our salvation.

LASCAUX

Every culture (or anyway every major urban/agricultural culture) cherishes two myths which apparently contradict each other: the myth of Degeneration & the myth of Progress. Réné Guénon & the neo-traditionalists like to pretend that no ancient culture ever believed in Progress, but of course they all did.

One version of the myth of Degeneration in Indo-European culture centers around the image of metals: gold, silver, bronze, iron. But what of the myth wherein Kronos & the Titans are destroyed to make way for Zeus & the Olympians? — a story which parallels that of Tiamat & Marduk, or Leviathan & Jah. In these "Progress" myths, an earlier chthonic chaotic earthbound (or watery) "feminine" pantheon is replaced (overthrown) by a later spiritualized orderly heavenly "male" pantheon. Is this not a *step forward* in Time? And have not Buddhism, Christianity, & Islam all claimed to be *better* than paganism?

In truth of course both myths — Degeneration as well as Progress — serve the purpose of Control & the Society of Control. Both admit that before the present state of affairs something else existed, a different form of the Social. In both cases we appear to be seeing a "race-memory" vision of the Paleolithic, the great long unchanging pre-history of the human. In one case that era is seen as a nastily brutish vast disorder; the 18th century did not *discover* this viewpoint, but found it already expressed in Classical & Christian culture. In the other case, the primordial is viewed as precious, innocent, happier, & easier than the present, more numinous than the present — but *irrevocably vanished*, impossible to recover except through death.

Thus for all loyal & enthusiastic devotees of Order, Order presents itself as immeasurably more perfect than any original Chaos; while for the disaffected potential enemies of Order, Order presents itself as cruel & oppressive ("iron") but utterly & fatally unavoidable — in fact, omnipotent.

In neither case will the mythopoets of Order admit that "Chaos" or "the Golden Age" could still exist in the present, or that they *do* exist in the present, here & now in fact — but repressed by the illusory totality of the Society of Order. We however believe that "the paleolithic" (which is neither more nor less a myth than "chaos" or "golden age") does exist even now as a kind of unconscious within the social. We also believe that as the Industrial Age comes to an end, & with it the last of the Neolithic "agricultural revolution," & with it the decay of the last religions of Order, that this "repressed material" will once again be uncovered. What else could we mean when we speak of "psychic nomadism" or "the disappearance of the Social"?

The end of the Modern does not mean a return TO the Paleolithic, but a return OF the Paleolithic.

Post-classical (or post-academic) anthropology has prepared us for this return of the repressed, for only very recently have we come to understand & sympathize with hunter/gatherer societies. The caves of Lascaux were rediscovered precisely when they needed to be rediscovered, for no ancient Roman nor medieval Christian nor 18th century rationalist could have ever have found them beautiful or significant. In these caves (symbols of an archaeology of consciousness) we found the artists who created them; we discovered them as ancestors, & also as *ourselves,* alive & present.

Paul Goodman once defined anarchism as "neolithic conservatism." Witty, but no longer accurate. Anarchism (or Ontological Anarchism, at least) no longer sympathizes with peasant agriculturalists, but with the non-authoritarian social structures & pre-surplus-value economics of the hunter/gatherers. Moreover we cannot describe this sympathy as "conservative." A better term would be "radical," since we have found our roots in the Old Stone Age, a kind of eternal present. We do not wish to return to a material technology of the past (we have no desire to bomb ourselves back to the Stone Age), but rather for the return of a psychic technology which we forgot we possessed.

The fact that we find Lascaux beautiful means that Babylon has at last begun to fall. Anarchism is probably more a symptom than a cause of this melting away. Despite our utopian imagination we do not know what to expect. But we, at least, are prepared for the *drift* into the unknown. For us it is an adventure, not the End of the World. We have welcomed the return of Chaos, for along with the danger comes —at last — a chance to create.

VERNISSAGE

What's so funny about *Art?*

Was Art laughed to death by dada? Or perhaps this sardonicide took place even earlier, with the first performance of *Ubu Roi?* Or with Baudelaire's sarcastic phantom-of-the-opera laughter, which so disturbed his good bourgeois friends?

What's funny about Art (though it's more funny-peculiar than funny-ha-ha) is the sight of the corpse that refuses to lie down, this zombie jamboree, this charnel puppetshow with all the strings attached to Capital (bloated Diego Rivera-style plutocrat), this moribund simulacrum jerking frenetically around, pretending to be the one single most truly alive thing in the universe.

In the face of an irony like this, a doubleness so extreme it amounts to an impassable abyss, any *healing* power of laughter-in-art can only be rendered suspect, the illusory property of a self-appointed elite or pseudo-avant-garde. To have a genuine avant-garde, Art must be *going somewhere,* & this has long since ceased to be the case. We mentioned Rivera; surely no more genuinely funny political artist has painted in our century — but in aid of what? Trotskyism! The deadest dead-end of twentieth century politics! No healing power *here* — only the hollow sound of powerless mockery, echoing over the abyss.

To heal, one first destroys — & political art which falls to destroy the target of its laughter ends by strengthening the very forces it sought to attack. "What doesn't kill me makes me stronger," sneers the porcine figure in its shiny top hat (mocking Nietzsche, of course, poor Nietzsche, who tried to laugh the whole nineteenth century to death, but ended up a living corpse, whose sister tied strings to his limbs to make him dance for fascists).

There's nothing particularly mysterious or metaphysical about the process. Circumstance, poverty, once forced Rivera to accept a commission to come to the USA & paint a mural — for Rockefeller! — the very archetypal Wall Street porker himself! Rivera made his work a blatant piece of Commie agitprop — & then Rockefeller had it *obliterated*. As if this weren't funny enough, the real joke is that Rockefeller could have savored victory even more sweetly by *not* destroying the work, but by paying for it & displaying it, turning it into Art, that toothless parasite of the interior decorator, that *joke*.

The dream of Romanticism: that the reality-world of bourgeois values could somehow be persuaded to consume, to take into itself, an art which at first seemed like all other art (books to read, paintings to hang on the wall, etc.), but which would secretly infect that reality with *something else*, which would change the way it saw itself, overturn it, replace it with the revolutionary values of art.

This was also the dream Surrealism dreamed. Even dada, despite its outward show of cynicism, still dared to hope. From Romanticism to Situationism, from Blake to 1968, the dream of each succeeding yesterday became the parlor decor of every tomorrow — bought, chewed, reproduced, sold, consigned to museums, libraries, universities, & other mausolea, forgotten, lost, resurrected, turned into nostalgia-craze, reproduced, sold, etc., etc., *ad nauseam*.

In order to understand how thoroughly Cruikshank or Daumier or Grandville or Rivera or Tzara or Duchamp *destroyed* the bourgeois worldview of their time, one must bury oneself in a blizzard of historical references &

hallucinate — for in fact the destruction-by-laughter was a theoretical success but an actual flop — the dead weight of illusion failed to budge even an inch in the gales of laughter, the *attack* of laughter. It wasn't bourgeois society which collapsed after all, it was art.

In the light of the trick which has been played on us, it appears to us as if the contemporary artist were faced with two choices (since suicide is *not* a solution): one, to go on launching attack after attack, movement after movement, in the hope that one day *(soon)* "the thing" will have grown so weak, so *empty*, that it will evaporate & leave us suddenly alone in the field; or, two, to begin *right now immediately* live as if the battle were already won, as if *today* the artist were no longer a special kind of person, but each person a special sort of artist. (This is what the Situationists called "the suppression & realization of art").

Both of these options are so "impossible" that to act on either of them would be a joke. We wouldn't have to make "funny" art because just making art would be funny enough to bust a gut. But at least it would be *our joke*. (Who can say for certain that we would fail? "I *love* not knowing the future" — Nietzsche. In order to begin to play this game, however, we shall probably have to set certain rules for ourselves:

1. There are no *issues*. There is no such thing as sexism, fascism, speciesism, looksism, or any other "franchise issue" which can be separated out from the social complex & treated with "discourse" as a "problem." There exists only the *totality* which subsumes all these illusory "issues" into the complete falsity of *its* discourse, thus rendering all opinions, pro & con, into mere thought-commodities to be bought & sold. And this *totality* is itself an illusion, an evil nightmare from which we are trying (through art, or humor, or by any other means) to awaken.

2. As much as possible whatever we do must be done outside the psychic/ economic structure set up by the *totality* as the permissible space for the game of art. How,

you ask, are we to make a living without galleries, agents, museums, commercial publishing, the NEA, & other welfare agencies of the arts? Oh well, one need not ask for the improbable. But one must indeed demand the "impossible" — or else why the fuck is one an artist?! It's not enough to occupy a special holy catbird seat called Art from which to mock at the stupidity & injustice of the "square" world. Art is part of the problem. The Art World has its head up its ass, & it has become necessary to disengage — or else live in a landscape full of shit.

3. Of course one must go on "making a living" somehow — but the essential thing is to make a life. Whatever we do, whichever option we choose (perhaps all of them), or however badly we compromise, we should pray never to mistake art for life: Art is brief, Life is long. We should try to be prepared to drift, to nomadize, to slip out of all nets, to never settle down, to live through many arts, to make our lives better than our art, to make art our boast rather than our excuse.

4. The healing laugh (as opposed to the poisonous & corrosive laugh) can only arise from an art which is serious — *serious* — *but not sober.* Pointless morbidity, cynical nihilism, trendy postmodern frivolity, whining/bitching/moaning (the liberal cult of the "victim"), exhaustion, Baudrillardian ironic hyperconformity — none of these options is *serious* enough, & at the same time none is *intoxicated* enough to suit our purposes, much less elicit our laughter.

"RAW VISION"

The categories of naive art, art brut, & insane or eccentric art, which shade into various & further categories of neo-primitive or urban-primitive art — all these ways of categorizing & labelling art remain senseless: — that is, not only ultimately useless but also essentially unsensual, unconnected to body & desire. What really characterizes all these art forms? Not their marginality in relation to a mainstream of art/discourse . . . for heaven's sake, what mainstream?! what discourse?! If we were to say that there's a "post-modernist" discourse currently going on, then the concept "margin" no longer holds any meaning. Post-post-modernism, however, will not even admit the existence of any discourse of any sort. Art has fallen silent. There are no more categories, much less maps of "center" & "margin." We are free of all that shit, right?

Wrong. Because one category survives: Capital. Too-Late Capitalism. The Spectacle, the Simulation, Babylon, whatever you want to call it. All art can be positioned or labelled in relation to this "discourse." And it is *precisely & only* in relation to this "metaphysical" commodity-spectacle that "outsider~ art can be seen as marginal. If this spectacle can be considered as a para-medium (in all its sinuous complexity), then "outsider" art must be called *im-mediate*. It does not pass thru the para-medium of the spectacle. It is meant only for the artist & the artist's "immediate entourage" (friends, family, neighbors, tribe); & it participates only in a "gift" economy of positive reciprocity. Only this non-category of

"Immediatism" can therefore approach an adequate understanding & defense of the *bodily* aspects of "outsider" art, its connection to the senses & to desire, & its avoidance or even ignorance of the mediation/ alienation inherent in spectacular recuperation & re- production. Mind you, this has nothing to do with the *content* of any outsider genre, nor for that matter does it concern the *form* or the intention of the work, nor the naivete or knowingness of the artist or recipients of the art. Its "Immediatism" lies solely in its means of *imaginal production*. It communicates or is "given" from person to person, "breast-to-breast" as the sufis say, without passing thru the distortion-mechanism of the spectacular para- medium.

   When Yugoslavian or Haitian or NYC-grafitti art was "discovered" & commodified, the results failed to *satisfy* on several points: — (1) in terms of the pseudo-discourse of the "Art World," all so-called "naivete" is doomed to remain quaint, even campy, & decidedly marginal — even when it commands high prices (for a year or two). The forced entrance of outsider art into the commodity spectacle is *a humiliation. (2)* Recuperation as commodity engages the artist in "negative reciprocity" — i.e., where first the artist "received inspiration" as a free gift, & then "made a donation" directly to other people, who might or might not "give back" their understanding, or mystification, or a turkey & a keg of beer (positive reciprocity), the artist now first creates for money & receives money, while any aspects of "gift" exchange recede into secondary levels of meaning & finally begin to fade (negative reciprocity). Finally we have *tourist* art, & the condescending amusement, & then the condescending boredom, of those who will no longer pay for the "inauthentic." (3) Or else the Art World vampirizes the energy of the outsider, sucks everything out & then passes on the corpse to the advertising world or the world of "popular" entertainment. By this *re- production* the art finally loses its "aura" & shrivels & dies.

True, the "utopian trace" may remain, but in essence the art has been *betrayed.*

The *unfairness* of such terms as "insane" or "neo-primitive" art lies in the fact that this art is not produced only by the mad or innocent, but by all those who evade the alienation of the para-medium. Its true appeal lies in the intense aura it acquires thru immediate imaginal *presence,* not only in its "visionary" style or content, but most importantly by its mere present-ness (i.e., it is "here" & it is a "gift"). In this sense it is more, not less, noble than "mainstream" art of the post-modern era — which is precisely the art of an absence rather than a presence.

The only *fair* way (or "beauty way," as the Hopi say) to treat "outsider" art would seem to be to keep it "secret" — to refuse to define it — to *pass it on* as a secret, person-to-person, breast-to-breast — rather than *pass it thru* the para-medium (slick journals, quarterlies, galleries, museums, coffee-table books, MTV, etc.). Or even better: — to become "mad" & "innocent" ourselves — for so Babylon will label us when we neither worship nor criticize it anymore — when we have *forgotten* it (but not "forgiven" it!), & remembered our own prophetic selves, our bodies, our "true will."

AN IMMEDIATIST POTLATCH

i.

Any number can play but the number must be pre-determined. Six to 25 seems about right.

ii.

The basic structure is a banquet or picnic. Each player must bring a dish or bottle, etc., of sufficient quantity that everyone gets at least a serving. Dishes can be prepared or finished on the spot, but nothing should be bought ready-made (except wine & beer, although these could ideally be home-made). The more elaborate the dishes the better. Attempt to be *memorable*. The menu need not be left to surprise (although this is an option) — some groups may want to coordinate the banquets so as to avoid duplications or clashes. Perhaps the banquet could have a theme & each player could be responsible for a given course (appetizer, soup, fish, vegetables, meat, salad, dessert, ices, cheeses, etc.). Suggested themes: Fourier's Gastrosophy — Surrealism — Native American — Black & Red (all food black or red in honor of anarchy) — etc.

iii.

The banquet should be carried out with a certain degree of formality: toasts, for example. Maybe "dress for dinner" in some way? (Imagine for example that the banquet theme were "Surrealism"; the concept "dress for dinner" takes on a certain meaning). Live music at the banquet would be fine, providing some of the players were content to perform for the others as their "gift," & eat later. (Recorded music is not appropriate.)

iv.

The main purpose of the potlatch is of course gift-giving. Every player should arrive with one or more gifts & leave with one or more *different* gifts. This could be accomplished in a number of ways: (a) Each player brings one gift & passes it to the person sealed next to them at table (or some similar arrangement); (b) Everyone brings a gift for *every* other guest. The choice may depend on the number of players, with (a) better for larger groups & (b) for smaller gatherings. If the choice is (b), you may want to decide beforehand whether the gifts should be the same or different. For example, if I am playing with five other people, do I bring (say) five hand-painted neckties, or five totally different gifts? And will the gifts be given specifically to certain individuals (in which case they might be crafted to suit the recipient's personality), or will they be distributed by lot?

v.

The gifts must be made by the players, not ready-made. This is vital. Premanufactured elements can go into the making of the gifts, but each gift must be an individual work of art in its own right. If for instance I bring five handpainted neckties, I must paint each one myself, either with the same or with different designs, although I may be allowed to buy ready-made ties to work on.

vi.

Gifts need not be physical objects. One player's gift might be live music during dinner, another's might be a performance. However, it should be recalled that in the Amerindian potlatches the gifts were supposed to be superb & even ruinous for the givers. In my opinion physical objects are best, & they should be *as good as possible* — not necessarily costly to make, but really impressive. Traditional potlatches involved prestige-winning. Players should feel a competitive spirit of giving, a determination to make gifts of real splendor or value. Groups may wish to set rules beforehand about this — some may wish to insist on physical objects, in which case music or performance would simply become extra acts of generosity, but *hors de potlatch,* so to speak.

vii.

Our potlatch is non-traditional, however, in that theoretically all players *win* — everyone gives & receives equally. There's no denying however that a dull or stingy player will lose prestige, while an imaginative and/or generous player will gain "face." In a really successful potlatch each player will be equally generous, so that all players will be equally pleased. The uncertainty of outcome adds a zest of randomness to the event.

viii.

The host, who supplies the place, will of course be put to extra trouble & expense, so that an ideal potlatch would be part of a series in which each player takes a turn as host. In this case another competition for prestige would transpire in the course of the series: — who will provide the most memorable hospitality? Some groups may want to set rules limiting the host's duties, while others may wish to leave hosts free to knock themselves out; however, in the latter case, there should really be a complete series of events, so that no one need feel cheated, or superior, in relation to the other players. But in some areas & for some groups the entire series may simply not be feasible. In New York for example not everyone has enough room to host even a small party. In this case the hosts will inevitably win some extra prestige. And why not?

ix.

Gifts should not be "useful." They should appeal to the senses. Some groups may prefer works of art, others might like home-made preserves & relishes, or gold frankincense & myrrh, or even sexual acts. Some ground rules should be agreed on. No mediation should be involved in the gift — no videotapes, tape recordings, printed material, etc. All gifts should be present at the potlatch "ceremony" — i.e. no tickets to other events, no promises, no postponements. Remember that the purpose of the game, as well as its most basic rule, is to avoid all mediation & even representation — to be *"present,"* to give *"presents."*

SILENCE

The problem is not that too much has been revealed, but that every revelation finds its sponsor, its CEO, its monthly slick, its clone Judases & replacement people.

You can't get sick from too much knowledge — but we *can* suffer from the virtualization of knowledge, its alienation from us & its replacement by a weird dull changeling or simulacrum — the same "data," yes, but now dead — like supermarket vegetables; no "aura."

Our malaise (January 1, 1992) arises from this: we hear not the language but the echo, or rather the reproduction ad infinitum of the language, its reflection upon a reflection-series of itself, even more self-referential & corrupt. The vertiginous perspectives of this VR datascape nauseate us because they contain no hidden spaces, no privileged opacities.

Infinite access to knowledge that simply fails to interact with the body or with the imagination — in fact the manichean ideal of fleshless soulless thought — modern media/politics as pure gnostic mentation, the anaesthetic ruminations of Archons & Aeons, suicide of the Elect . . .

The organic is secretive — it secretes secrecy like sap. The inorganic is a demonic democracy — everything equal, but equally valueless. No gifts, only commodities. The Manichaeans invented usury. Knowledge can act as a kind of poison, as Nietzsche pointed out.

Within the organic ("Nature," "everyday life") is embedded a kind of silence which is not just dumbness, an opacity which is not mere ignorance — a secrecy which is also an affirmation — a tact which knows how to act, how to change things, how to breathe into them.

Not a "cloud of unknowing" — not "mysticism" — we have no desire to deliver ourselves up again to that obscurantist sad excuse for fascism — nevertheless we might invoke a sort of taoist sense of "suchness-of-things" — "a flower does not talk," & it's certainly not the genitals which endow us with logos. (On second thought, perhaps this is not quite true; after all, myth offers us the archetype of Priapus, a talking penis.) An occultist would ask how to "work" this silence — but we'd rather ask how to play it, like musicians, or like the playful boy of Heraclitus.

A bad mood in which every day is the same. When are a few lumps going to appear in this smooth time? Hard to believe in the return of Carnival, of Saturnalia. Perhaps time has stopped here in the Pleroma, here in the Gnostic dreamworld where our bodies are rotting but our "minds" are downloaded into eternity. We know so much — how can we not know the answer to this most vexing of questions?

Because the answer (as in Odilon Redon's "Harpocrates") isn't answered in the language of reproduction but in that of gesture, touch, odor, the hunt. Finally *virtu* is impassable — eating & drinking is eating & drinking — the lazy yokel plows a crooked furrow. The Wonderful World of Knowledge has turned into some kind of PBS Special from Hell. I demand real mud in my stream, real watercress. Why, the natives are not only sullen, they're taciturn — downright incommunicative. Right, gringo, we're tired of your steenking surveys, tests & questionnaires. There are some things bureaucrats were not meant to know — & so there are some things which even artists should keep secret. This is not self-censorship nor self-ignorance. It is cosmic tact. It is our homage to the organic, its uneven flow, its backcurrents & eddies, its swamps & hideouts. If art is "work" then it will become knowledge &

eventually lose its redemptive power & even its taste. But if art is "play" then it will both preserve secrets & tell secrets which will remain secrets. Secrets are for sharing, like all of Nature's secretions. Is knowledge *evil?* We're no mirror-image Manichees here — we're counting on dialectics to break a few bricks. Some knowledge is dadata, some is commodata. Some knowledge is wisdom — some simply an excuse for doing nothing, desiring nothing. Mere academic knowledge, for example, or the knowingness of the nihilist post-mods, shades off into realms of the UnDead—& the UnBorn. Some knowledge breathes — some knowledge suffocates. What we know & how we know it must have a basis in the flesh — the whole flesh, not just a brain in a jar of formaldehyde. The knowledge we want is neither utilitarian nor "pure" but celebratory. Anything else is a totentanz of data-ghosts, the "beckoning fair ones" of the media, the Cargo Cult of too-Late Capitalist epistemology.

If I could escape this bad mood of course I'd do so, & take you with me. What we need is a plan. Jail break? tunnel? a gun carved of soap, a sharpened spoon, a file in a cake? a new religion?

Let me be your wandering bishop. We'll play with the silence & make it ours. Soon as Spring comes. A rock in the stream, bifurcating its turbulence. Visualize it: mossy, wet, viridescent as rainy jadefaded copper struck by lightning. A great toad like a living emerald, like Mayday. The strength of the *bios,* like the strength of the bow or lyre, lies in the *bending back.*

CRITIQUE OF THE LISTENER

To speak too much & not be heard — that's sickening enough. But to acquire *listeners* — that could be worse. Listeners think that to listen suffices — as if their true desire were to hear with someone else's ears, see thru someone else's eyes, feel with someone else's skin . . .

The text (or the broadcast) which will change reality: — Rimbaud dreamed of that & then gave up in disgust. But he entertained too subtle an idea about magic. The crude truth is perhaps that texts can only change reality when they inspire readers to *see & act,* rather than merely *see.* Scripture once did this — but Scripture has become an idol. To see thru its eyes would be to possess (in the Voodoo sense) a statue — or a corpse.

Seeing, & the literature of seeing, is too easy. Enlightenment is easy. "It's easy to be a sufi," a Persian shaykh once told me. What's difficult is to be human. Political enlightenment is even easier than spiritual enlightenment — neither one changes the world or even the self. Sufism & Situationism — or shamanism & anarchy — the theories I've played with — are just that: theories, visions, ways of seeing. Significantly, the practice of sufism consists in the repetition of words (dhikr). This action itself is a text, & nothing but a text. And the "praxis" of anarcho-situationism amounts to the same: a text, a slogan on a wall. A moment of enlightenment. Well it's not totally valueless — but afterwards what will be *different?*

We might like to purge our radio of anything which lacks at least the *chance* of precipitating that difference.

Just as there exist books which have inspired earthshaking crimes we would like to broadcast texts which cause hearers to seize (or at least make a grab for) the happiness God denies us. Exhortations to hijack reality. But even more we would like to purge our lives of everything which obstructs or delays us from setting out — not to sell guns & slaves in Abyssinia — not to be either robbers or cops — not to escape the world or to rule it — but to open ourselves to difference.

I share with the most reactionary moralists the presumption that art can really affect reality in this way, & I despise the liberals who say all art should be permitted because — after all — it's only art. Thus I've taken to the practice of those categories of writing & radio most hated by conservatives — pornography & agitprop — in the hope of stirring up trouble for my readers/hearers & myself. But I accuse myself of ineffectualism, even futility. Not enough has changed. Perhaps nothing has changed.

Enlightenment is all we have, & even that we've had to rip from the grasp of corrupt gurus & bumbling suicidal intellectuals. As for our art — what have we accomplished, other than to spill our blood for the ghostworld of fashionable ideas & images?

Writing has taken us to the very edge beyond which writing may be impossible. Any texts which could survive the plunge over this edge — into whatever abyss or Abyssinia lies beyond — would have to be virtually self-created, like the miraculous hidden-treasure Dakini-scrolls of Tibet or the tadpole-script spirit-texts of Taoism — & absolutely incandescent, like the last screamed messages of a witch or heretic burning at the stake (to paraphrase Artaud).

I can sense these texts trembling just beyond the veil.

What if the mood should strike us to renounce both the mere objectivity of art & the mere subjectivity of theory? to risk the abyss? What if no one followed? So much the better, perhaps — we might find our equals amongst the Hyperboreans. What if we went mad? Well — that's the risk. What if we were bored? Ah . . .

Already some time ago we placed all our bets on the irruption of the marvelous into everyday life — won a few, then lost heavily. Sufism was indeed much much easier. Pawn everything then, down to the last miserable scrawl? double our stakes? cheat?

It's as if there were angels in the next room beyond thick walls — arguing? fucking? One can't make out a single word.

Can we retrain ourselves at this late date to become Finders of hidden treasure? And by what technique, seeing that it is precisely technique which has betrayed us? Derrangement of the senses, insurrection, piety, poetry? *Knowing how* is a cheap mountebank's trick. But *knowing what* might be like divine self-knowledge — it might create *ex nihilo*.

Finally, however, it will become necessary to leave this city which hovers immobile on the edge of a sterile twilight, like Hamelin after all the children were lured away. Perhaps other cities exist, occupying the same space & time, but . . . different. And perhaps there exist jungles where mere enlightenment is outshadowed by the black light of jaguars. I have no idea — & I'm terrified.

Some Recent Titles from AK Press

WHICH WAY FOR THE ECOLOGY MOVEMENT by Murray Bookchin; ISBN 1 873176 26 0; 80pp two color cover, perfect bound 5-1/2 x 8-1/2; £4.50/$6.00. Bookchin attacks the misanthropic notions that the environmental crisis is caused mainly by overpopulation or humanity's genetic makeup. He points to the social and economic causes as the problem the environmental movement must deal with.

TELEVISIONARIES: THE RED ARMY FACTION STORY 1963 TO 1993 by Tom Vague; ISBN 1 873176 47 3; 112pp two color cover; perfect bound 5-1/2 x 8-1/2; £4.50/$6.95. An irreverent chronological history and analysis of the terrorist group that have shot and bombed their way through the last three decades. From student radicalism to Stammheim to Euroterrorism, this is the only book in print which charts the raise and raise of the armed guerilla group that launched 1,000 t-shirts.

TESTCARD F: TELEVISION, MYTHINFORMATION AND SOCIAL CONTROL constructed by Anonymous; ISBN 1 873176 91 0; 80 pp four color cover, perfect bound 5-1/2 x 8-1/2; £4.50/$6.00. Using savage image-text cut and paste, this book explodes all previous media theory and riots through the Global Village, looting the ideological supermarket of all its products.

END TIME: NOTES ON THE APOCALYPSE by G.A. Matiasz; ISBN 1873176 96 1; 320 pp four color cover, perfect bound 5-1/2 x 8-1/2; £5.95/$7.00. A first novel by G.A. Matiasz, an original voice of slashing, thought provoking style. "A compulsively readable thriller combined with a very smart meditation on the near-future of anarchism, *End Time* proves once again that science fiction is our only literature of ideas." — Hakim Bey

ECSTATIC INCISIONS: THE COLLAGES OF FREDDIE BAER by Freddie Baer, preface by Peter Lamborn Wilson; ISBN 1 873176 60 0; 80 pages, a three color cover, perfect bound 8 1/2 x 11; £7.95/$11.95. This is Freddie Baer's first collection of collage work; over the last decade her illustrations have appeared on numerous magazine covers, posters, t-shirts, and album sleeves. Includes collaborations with Hakim Bey, T. Fulano, Jason Keehn, and David Watson.

STEALWORKS: THE GRAPHIC DETAILS OF JOHN YATES by John Yates; ISBN 1 873176 51 1; 136 pp two color cover, perfect bound 8-1/2 x 11; £7.95/$11.95. A collection to date of work created by a visual mechanic and graphic surgeon. His work is a mixture of bold visuals, minimalist to-the-point social commentary, involves the manipulation and reinterpretation of culture's media imagery.

AK Press publishes and distributes a wide variety of radical literature. For our latest catalog featuring these and several thousand other titles, please send a large self-addressed, stamped envelope to:

AK Press
22 Lutton Place
Edinburgh, Scotland
EH8 9PE, Great Britain

AK Press
P.O. Box 40682
San Francisco, CA
94140-0682